The Gift *of the* Magi:
Christmas for a New Millennium

1134/2000

The Gift *of the* Magi:
Christmas for a New Millennium

Rick Merlin Levine

Illustrated by Rhonda Eklund

Special Limited Edition
November, 1997

The Gift of the Magi: Christmas for a New Millenium
Copyright © 1997 by Rick Merlin Levine
Illustrated by Rhonda Eklund

ISBN 0-9654887-0-5

.

Levine, Rick
A fascinating look at the astrological origins of Christmas, the
role of the Magi, and the meaning of the Star of Bethlehem.
Poetry.

1. Christmas   2. Jesus Christ   3. Astrology   4. Poetry

16149 Redmond Way, Suite 288
Redmond, WA 98052

(425) 882-3481

email spellbound@verycosmic.com
http://www.verycosmic.com/spellbound/

"Now when Jesus was born in Bethlehem of Judaea in the days of Herod the king, behold, there came wise men from the east to Jerusalem, saying, where is he that is born King of the Jews? For we have seen his star in the east, and are come to worship him." (Matthew 2:1,2)

"The birth of Jesus Christ, the Bible says, was marked by the appearance of a star. This star attracted wise men—devout men—from the East. It led them to journey to a remote desert place, where the baby Jesus was.

Historians have concluded that this *star* was likely a remarkably strong light, caused by the alignment of the planets Jupiter and Saturn..." *Christian Science Monitor* (December 20, 1995)

*Dedicated to all those who have raised their eyes
toward the heavens to better understand
the web of relationships between
the divine and the human.*

Acknowledgments

I am grateful for the encouragement of many people, both family and friends, who have read my Christmas poems over the years. Without this encouragement, this book would have never happened. I am also grateful for the many people over the years who have shared their research about the Star of Bethlehem with me. I would like to acknowledge Percy Semour, who in *Astrology: The Evidence of Science* addressed many of the same issues that I address here. I'd also like to acknowledge Maria Kay Simms and Neil Michelsen, who in *Search for the Christmas Star,* retell the Christmas story from an astrological point of view. I want to thank Paul Roberts, author of *In Search of the Birth of Jesus,* whose book added new dimensions to my understanding of the times of Jesus and of the Zoroastrian culture. I am also grateful to Noel Tyl, who has encouraged my poetic lean for many years and who told me that if I didn't publish this book now, I would miss a great window of opportunity. Thank you, Noel. I would also like to acknowledge the editorial and proofreading assistance of Lori Eagle and Beth Coppermayr. And of course no writing project of mine would seem complete without the caring eyes of Heidi Rain. But most of all, I am deeply indebted to Rhonda Eklund, extraordinary visionary artist, who got the vision and took the time to create the amazing illustrations that grace the cover and the pages of this book. Thank you, Rhonda, for being a part of this project, and for being a part of my life. Your pictures have truly brought my words to life.

Preface

The Star of Bethlehem signaled the arrival of the baby Jesus and a new age on earth. This light that shone for a brief moment, twenty centuries ago, still captures the minds and hearts of our modern culture. What was its magic? Of what relevance today is the story of the origins of Christianity?

Two thousand years ago, according to our best historical recollections, three wise men looked toward the heavens, toward the reality of God. They saw something that transformed them, something that gave them a new perspective. They saw a wondrous new star, the very same one predicted by the old prophets. The wise men began a long journey that culminated in the recognition of a child who was destined to change history. The light that was seen by the Three Wise Men was a heavenly portent of the Age of Christianity. But the Star of Bethlehem was not easily noticeable. The Wise Men had to take King Herod into the night and point it out to him so that he could see it.

Now, in these modern times, once again, the light that appeared as a miracle star over Bethlehem has appeared in our skies, *and only those who are shown its glory can see the wonder of it all!*

Every year, during the deepening and darkening days of winter, in homes around the globe, the miracle of the Star of Bethlehem is revisited. The miracle of this star is the magic of hope. It is the wonder of every newborn baby, with godliness and perfection, not tampered yet by human failings and the gravity of life.

We stand again at a crossroads of history. The light that shone once as the Star of Bethlehem again signals the arrival of a new time, a time of human evolution, a time for humankind, a time for peace, a time of understanding. Though that light is now dimmed, it will most certainly have its day. Unfortunately, the purity of that light is now obscured, hidden by the dark powers of those who take without giving, who thirst after money and power. A battle is raging. Winner takes all... either the human race will be broken by its own techno-hysterical greed and will lay wasted alongside crumbled civilizations and a destroyed planet, or we'll have one more chance to regain paradise here on earth.

At this very special time in history, there are great changes under foot. These are times of mythical proportions. Pre-2000 humanity is at the gateway to a new millennium. Two thousand years ago, the gift of the magi was a miracle. It was a sign from the heavens that there was new hope. Political events were dismal as they are now. Times were serious. The end seemed near.

In this book, we will see that the gift of the magi is a gift for today. The gift of the magi gives us another chance for success in the universe. As we journey around again on this cosmic merry-go-round, it's time to reach for the golden ring.

The golden ring—we've waited for eternity. Now, it is so very close, yet apparently still just beyond our reach. So we must stretch our minds a bit further. Stretch, and the dream is yours. The dream is our shared dream, for now, with the advent of electronic media, humankind shares the same dreams. We are each a variation on a theme, the theme of life. Each of us plays our own individual variation on the cosmic theme... in different keys, different rhythms, different colors, different languages, different times and spaces.

The light of Christmas is eternal. The light of the Star of Bethlehem is shining again! We have another chance, another time around, and another golden ring.

This book is a collection of visions based upon the Christmas story. There is no doubt that there were three wise men, Zoroastrian magi from Persia and that they studied the stars. By weaving the story of the Star of Bethlehem with a juxtaposition of ancient and modern astrology, we arrive at a fresh new way of looking at modern events.

Three astrologers saw his special star rise.
They knew when to act; what made them so wise?

They knew, you see, to watch for the signs.
They knew what was up; they tuned in to their times.

Today, there's much to get distracted by,
We can't be too lazy; we all have to try
To hold on to our center in the midst of it all;
To watch for the signs and to heed the call
Of the path leading to greater heights;
To embrace the downtrodden in their basic fights;
To worship our God in our own unique style,
And to live life to the fullest while wearing a smile;
To smile within 'cause we know in our heart
That we each are important as we each play our part.

My part includes writing this poem
That has found its way into your home.

This book has words for you and for yours
To read while you take a break from chores;
To ride on my words, however trite;
To know that I send you with all my might
A wish for you and the ones that you love;
That you may be granted by the stars up above
A year of growth and a year of good health,
A year of emotional and spiritual wealth,
And on my words, however contrived
You'll know that a special poem has arrived.

Now it's the season of good will and bright cheer
With Hanukkah, Christmas, and the New Year—

No matter your religious or political stands
You can see change spread throughout all the lands;
We each must now find a place in our heart;
By spreading peace, we each do our part.

The lesson of the Christmas star:
It matters not how small you are.

So, as waves of change lap at our shores
I sing Happy Holidays to you and yours.

Rick Levine,
Redmond, Washington 1997

The Star *of* Bethlehem

Although Christmas is a holy day in the Christian tradition, it has become even more than a Christian holiday. The Christmas season has become infused into our culture everywhere we look. At this time of year, it really doesn't matter whether you're Jewish, Muslim, Christian, Hindu, or Buddhist. During the deepening of winter, the Christmas spirit permeates the air.

The story of the Christmas Star is enshrouded in mystery. There are things that are illusion and there are things that are real. We're taught through religious metaphor that something very magical happened at the time of this star. There was a signal from God, a brilliance in the heavens that stopped people in their tracks. It signified the Holy of Holies. As we look back through historical records, however, we realize that no one even noticed this awesome event. No one, that is, except for some Persian magi. The Chinese have been avid sky watchers for thousands of years. They recorded comets and novae, yet they didn't notice anything in the sky at that time. Other cultures didn't record anything either. So the question is, *if there was a magical star really shining in the heavens, why didn't everyone notice?*

The Bible tells us that Three Wise Men were present to witness the birth of the baby Jesus. Newer translations correctly identify these three cosmically invited guests as astrologers. The word *magi* has the same origination as the word magician, not to be confused here with a modern stage magician or entertainer. Magi is used interchangeably with *wise men*. Just as *rabbi* is the title of a Jewish teacher, so *magus* is the title of a Zoroastrian priest.

Zoroastrianism

Far to the east of Israel is the magical, mystical land of India. Between India and the Holy Land is an area that was, in ancient times, called Chaldea. Chaldea was the home of a great and ancient sacred knowledge called astrology. Chaldea became Babylon, which later became Persia. Five centuries before the birth of Jesus, the prophet Zoroaster brought a new religion to this land. Zoroastrianism played a significant role in this ancient world. Zoroastrian priests were *astronomer-priests*. The ancient Persian temples, ziggurats, were astronomical observatories. In these observatory-temples, the ancient Persian priests spent the nights watching the divine magic unfold. Around the time of the Jesus' birth, Zoroastrian magi undoubtedly practiced astrology. They carefully watched the movements of peculiar stars that seemed to wander through the zodiac. These *wandering stars,* that we now call planets, helped them better understand events on earth.

The ancient astronomical mindset

To reconstruct the mindset of several thousand years ago, we must look at the word *star.* Stars are hot gases, like our Sun. There are many kinds of stars, including neutron stars, red giants, blue dwarfs, black holes, binary stars, quasars, and pulsars. Stars are basically nuclear *reactors,* giving off light energy, as does our own yellow Sun. What kind of star was the Christmas Star? As represented in literature and in illustrations, the Christmas Star has always been shown as some sort of brilliant supernova. Stars have been historically recorded to be so bright that they were even seen during daylight hours! But the Christmas star was not recorded like that. Remember, it was not observed outside of Persia. A star was anything in the sky that gave off light.

To the ancient scientists who looked up, the planets were stars. Today, we think of a planet as a body that goes around the sun, but to the ancients, the word *planet* meant "star that wanders." Some stars wandered. Some stars were fixed. But they were all stars.

The astrological metaphor in ancient times was deeply ingrained. Everything was integrated and connected. The things that happened in the heavens corresponded to the same events on Earth. The astronomer priests were considered amongst the wisest people of their time because they knew how to read the signs in the divine realms of the night sky.

The original Aramaic text quotes the magi as saying they had seen "his star in *heliacal* rising." Heliacal rising means that it is the last star that is seen in the sky before the sun rises and makes the other stars invisible in the brightness of daylight. This was a common observation technique for astrologers of those days.

In astrology, the slowest moving planets are the most serious of the celestial wanderers. Slower moving planets have the most impact upon earthly events. The ancient astrologers observed the apparent movement of the sun, the moon, Mercury, Venus, Mars, Jupiter, and Saturn against the backdrop of the fixed stars in the zodiac. All these *wanderers* were visible to the naked eye. It would be centuries before the telescope would bring additional planets into view. The greatest planetary rhythm that was observable to the ancient astronomer-priest was the rhythm of the Jupiter/Saturn conjunction. A conjunction occurs when two planets line up on their individual journeys around the sun. The Jupiter/Saturn conjunction is a regular planetary rhythm that happens every twenty years. However, because of its peculiar nature, it actually jumps from astrological sign to sign with great regularity. Although Jupiter and Saturn align every twenty years, the movement of this alignment through the zodiac is a centuries-long process. It is the combination of astrologically rare events that created the Star of Bethlehem.

The King's Star and the Star of David

There is much evidence to suggest that what we call the Star of David was an alignment of the giant planets Jupiter and Saturn. In ancient Jewish tradition, Jupiter was the planet called the "King's Star." Even later in Greek mythology, Jupiter, or Jove, was the King of the Gods. Every 20 years, when the King's Star lined up with Saturn, the star of final authority, the ancient Jews called this *The Star of David*.

Christ is a Greek word for king. A king was one who was literally born under the cosmic signature of the King's Star. Jesus, as we know, was born in the lineage of the House of David. But to be born in the lineage of David didn't only mean that you had parents in that lineage. It also meant that you were born under the Star of David, *which occurred when Jupiter, the King's Star, aligned with Saturn.*

Johannes Kepler

Fifteen centuries after the birth of Jesus, German-born Johannes Kepler enters our story. Kepler is considered the "Father of Modern Astronomy." He was also a brilliant astrologer. He uncovered the mathematics of the cosmos and discovered the *Laws of Planetary Motion*. He also figured out the recurring patterns of conjunctions for Jupiter and Saturn.

Personally moved by his own observation of a Jupiter/Saturn conjunction in 1603, just before Christmas, Kepler mused over the meaning of the Christmas star. He did some calculations and figured out that there was a Jupiter/Saturn conjunction in the years 7 and 6 BC.

Although Jupiter and Saturn reach conjunction every twenty years, on occasion they actually conjunct three times within a year, from earth's point of view. This phenomena is called a triple conjunction. According to Kepler's calculations, there was, in fact, a triple conjunction of Jupiter and Saturn, in the sign of Pisces, in the years 7-6 BC. Kepler also learned from the writings of a medieval scholar, Rabbi Abarbonel, the extreme importance of the Jupiter/Saturn conjunction in the sign of Pisces for the Jewish people. This whole concept intrigued Johannes Kepler. So Kepler was the first person of our era to realize that the Star of Bethlehem was a lineup of Jupiter and Saturn, based upon an Old Testament prophecy of the coming of the King of Kings. The Prophets said that the arrival of this messiah would be associated with a celestial event as a sign from God.

The Grand Mutation

In the decades prior to the birth of Jesus, there was renewed talk of a New World Order. The fervor of the times was that the Coming of the Kingdom of God was at hand! For centuries prior to this changeful period of history, there was a belief that a Messiah, a great teacher, would herald a new age on earth. This prophecy told of an apocalypse, a reversal of everything that was known. To better understand this prophecy, we should realize that ancient astrology had different signs associated with different peoples of that time. The sign associated with the Hebrews was the sign of Pisces, the Fish. As the Jupiter/Saturn conjunction moves through its regular pattern around the zodiac, this is called the "Grand Mutation Cycle." The Jupiter/Saturn conjunction of 7-6 BC in Pisces was, in fact, a Grand Mutation. This Grand Mutation was destined to be a harbinger of the New Age, the age we would later call *The Age of Christianity*. Jesus of Nazareth was not *just* born under a King's Star. He was born under a highly propitious King's Star alignment in the Sign of Pisces, the very sign of the Jews!

The changing of the ages

The word *age* is a very specific astrological word. An age is the time that it takes the Earth's axis to precess through one sign of the zodiac. If you spin a top, it start to wobble backwards as it slows down. The spin rotates one way, yet the wobble moves the opposite way the top is spinning. The Earth does this, too. It wobbles like a top. The Earth is spinning around one way, and also wobbling backwards. The earth's polar axis completes one full wobble once every 25,920 years. This backward wobble of the North Pole creates what astrologers call the *Precession of the Equinox*.

Every 72 years at the first moment of spring, the vernal equinox point slips backward against the zodiac by one degree. Every 2160 years it slips back 30°, or one whole sign of the astrological zodiac.

For the last couple of thousand years, the North Pole of the Earth has been pointing to that area in the sky we call Pisces. This means that, astrologically, we have been in the *Age of Pisces*, or the *Age of the Fish!* Note the connections between the fish and Christianity. Christ was a fisher among men. The *vesica Pisces,* the vessel of the soul, became a symbol for the church. Fish represents the apparent multiplicity, and in the Age of the Fish, it was reserved for the religious mystic to see how all the individual fishes are, in truth, one.

In these times, we have talk now of another new age, *The Age of Aquarius.* Because the equinox slips *backwards*, it goes from Pisces to Aquarius, rather than Aries. It is the resonance between the changing of the ages two thousand years ago, and the changing of the ages in modern times that captures our attention as this story unfolds.

Historical perspectives

But what makes us believe that Jesus was really born under this astrologically significant star, even if this story sounds plausible? Is there any evidence that the birth was in 7 or 6 BC? Is it possible that our whole calendar is wrong?

Josephus, a well-known Roman historian, wrote about 70-80 years after the birth of Jesus. Josephus kept detailed records, and from them we can get a record of those times.

In the Roman Empire, tax collection happened approximately every 14 years. The tax involved a census. Josephus records a call for a tax collection in 8 BC. Since Joseph was of the tribe of David, he had to return to Bethlehem, his home town. It may have taken several months or even a year to go from one end of the country to the other. This chronology places Joseph and Mary in Bethlehem around 8 BC.

King Herod also plays a role in identifying the chronology of the birth of Jesus. We know that King Herod was alive at the time of Jesus' birth, for the Bible tells us that the three magi were called to his court on their journey to Bethlehem. A couple of years after the birth of Jesus, a fearful Herod called for the murdering of all of the male children in the Bethlehem area who were less than 2 years old. He wanted to be sure no "King of Kings" would ever usurp his power as King of Judaea. The records of Josephus also tell us that Herod died during a lunar eclipse in April, and although Josephus doesn't tell us the year, we do know there was a lunar eclipse in April of 4 BC.

We can therefore surmise that Jesus' birth might have been sometime after 8 BC and before 4 BC, but our calendar still tells us something different. Why? Because the birth date for Jesus of Nazareth was not established until five centuries later.

The ancients kept time by local calendars. Time was kept with a terminology called AUC (*ad urba condida*) which means "from the founding of the city." Every city had its own calendar, and when a new conquering empire took control, the local calendars were reset.

Around 530 AD, the Pope assigned to a monk named Dionysius Exigiuus the task of setting the date for the origin of the calendar. The calendar was to begin with the birth of Jesus. Dionysius came up short of his task on at least two counts that we know of. First, he assigned the year 1 to the time of the birth. This doesn't allow for the year from zero to one! Second, he calculated that Jesus was born in the year 754 AUC, using the local calendar in Bethlehem at the time. Dionysius uncovered a four hundred-year-old chronology that showed that Jesus was born during the reign of Caesar Augustus. He figured that the 28th year of Augustus' reign was when Jesus was born, but he missed the significant fact that Augustus ruled for four years the name Octavian! With the year for the year zero, plus the four additional years, our calendar is at *least five years off!*

Although our calendar is set by the birth of Jesus, it is evident that there Jesus was not born in the year 0001. Our modern calendar is wrong!

Origins of Christianity

The gift of the magi was really the gift of the changing of civilization. It doesn't matter what religion you are, the last two thousand years have been the age of Christianity.

The magi are so central to the Christmas story that in the Eastern Orthodox Church, Epiphany celebrates the arrival of the gift-bearing magi at the birth place of the baby Jesus. The Three Wise Men sought out the birth of a baby to play a role in the founding of a religion that has been dominant for two thousand years. The birth of Jesus may have been the single most important event in the last two thousand years, because it so altered the course of history worldwide. The magi were the first people who recognized the event. If these astrologers hadn't properly identified that event, apparently no one would have even known that there was a star!

The suppressed origins of Christianity date back to these magi who recognized the signs of their times. The magi showed the sign of the Star of Bethlehem to King Herod, and he was amazed and he became fearful of the power of change. The magi were undoubtedly the founders of Christmas, and to some extent the founders of Christianity.

The Cult of Mithras

There is much more to the origins of Christianity than we are taught. The historical record is very clear, showing us traditions that were already in place at the time of Jesus. Mithraism, well-documented and paralleling the story of Jesus and the church, was a Roman cult that preceded Christianity by centuries. The story tells of Mithras, miraculously born of a virgin birth at the Winter Solstice, under an auspicious star. Mithras was greeted with gifts from shepherds. He acted as a mediator between man and supreme being, sent to earth as a flesh representation of God. He fought to preserve the world from an evil one, the fallen angel, ascended into heaven at the spring equinox, which is when we still celebrate the resurrection. Mithras partook of a last supper of bread and wine with twelve disciples, and presided over a hierarchy of believers who addressed each other as brother. They were even led in a congregation by a Father under a hierarchy of Fathers, who lived in Rome. The Father of Fathers in Rome was known as "Papa." They served cakes marked with the sign of the cross at ritual feasts. Mithras was honored on the seventh day, rather than the sixth day, which was the *Saturn*day that the Jews worshipped. The Seventh day was the *Sun*day. Mithras rescued mankind from a great flood by teaching one man how to build an ark. Mithras was worshipped in elaborate circles with beautifully dressed priests wearing mitres, and it is from that word mitre that Mithras came. A mitre is a pointed hat. The Cult of Mithras was the Cult of the Pointed Hat. This hat is the very same hat that is still worn by the Pope! So we see that the story of Jesus corresponded to traditions already in place. And a great teacher came along to act as a catalyzing agent, bringing these disparate traditions into a singular new religion that took the world by storm.

Cosmic alignments then and now

The story of the Star of Bethlehem tells us that cosmic alignments herald earthly events. The Lord's Prayer tells us that "it is done on earth as it is in heaven." The words are clear even if we, in our scientific mindset, shirk from the true meaning. Ancient prophecy was often astrological.

Today modern scientists are rediscovering the meaning of cosmic cycles and their effects upon life on earth. The 1960s were an explosive and changeful decade. According to our modern astrologers, the sixties were defined by the powerful alignment of Uranus and Pluto. This "star" could never have been known by the ancients, for the outer planets have only been discovered in the past couple of centuries, but modern astrologers have traced this conjunction back through history and have retrospectively observed the cultural upheaval that it brings.

Within a relatively short cosmic span, we again experienced another very rare "star." In the late eighties and early nineties, astrologers observed a most rare alignment of three slow-moving planets. Saturn aligned with Uranus *and* Neptune, something which only happens every 684 years! That this rare event happened in the same lifetime as the Uranus/Pluto conjunction of the sixties creates a time of unprecedented political and religious change. Everyone feels like we are on the edge of something, but no one knows what it is. There's talk of new kinds of energy, new healing paradigms, possibilities of powerful new technologies. Change is happening faster than ever before. Fact is confused with imagination, and the two seem inseparable.

Christmas is a magical time of year. Time collapses from the ancient through the present. We remind ourselves about what was happening thousands of years ago, and these events still have relevance today.

It is almost like the biblical flood is happening again, but this time the flood waters aren't falling from the sky as rain. Instead we are being deluged with invisible and subtle electromagnetic vibrations falling from the sky. These high frequency waves are alive with information. This is a flood of emotion, a flood of data and a flood of images. We each contend with this flood. Like Noah, we have our own individual arks. But in this flood of metaphysical images, we build non-physical, spiritual arks to help us ride the wild cultural tidal currents.

What will the stars of the late 20th Century mean to the big historical picture? What will these times bring? The Christmas Star brings us an answer, or at least a perspective. Even if we were alive during the ministry of Jesus and were personally touched by his spiritual magic, we could not, in our wildest imagination, have predicted what was to follow. By the same token, even if we accept that these are times of great proportion, and that we are at the edge of a new world, we cannot know what is around the bend of history.

All we can do is pay attention to what is happening and uncover as much truth as we can about our past. All we can do is remind ourselves and those close to us that love is stronger than fear, and that truth is more powerful than deception.

> *The message of the Christmas Star:*
> *It matters not how small you are.*
> *When truth and love are shared with all*
> *Nothing that we do is small.*

One

I just heard the news from a wise old sage,
He told me of the coming age.
A new time on earth, a different order;
He said we're ready to cross the border,
Like crossing a river into a new land,
Now we're crossing through time (just as planned).

Ages change every two thousand years.
This fact's been known by prophetic seers.
The last age was marked by the birth of a child.
The times were terrible, the event was so mild.
The simple life of a Rabbi, Jesus his name,
Upset the elders. Heresy was his game.
Truth, as he lived it, came from his tongue.
Love and forgiveness was the song that he sung.
Truth, as he knew it, shined from his heart.
He walked through his life as he played out his part.

But the Jews and the Romans just would not accept
His radical teachings, so the old ways they kept.

In matters of change, there's no right or wrong,
You do what you must, and be where you belong,
But some things go down that make us react,
That change things a lot, and that's just a fact!

So whether we're Hindu or Moslem or Jew
Christmas is not just a time for a few
Christians to celebrate an event from the past.
It's a time to remember great changes that last!

Time's funny. It circles. It zigs and it zags.
We now live in times of riches and rags
In an era of truly amazing contrast
Where the pace of life is incredibly fast;
Where the Global Village has gotten so small
That time and space seem non-existent at all;
Where so much each day happens all over the earth,
We forget the importance of each little birth,
But each child born so new and unique
Is like a messiah – the savior we seek.

If we accept that children, in divine image are made,
Do we wish them to live in the world we have made?
Cannot we attempt to clean up the air
Of all excess hostilities that we have put there?
Destroying our weapons of anger and hate
Would bring peace on earth. *It's never too late!*

In this Holiday Season of gift-buying acts,
I'd like you to think of a couple of facts.
The gurus and prophets and seers and sages
All say it's now time for the changing of ages
And we, in our wisdom, how'er wise we are,
We don't understand the life of a star...

The universe is quite a fantastic place
Where time is just as confusing as space.
We get so involved with our narrow concern
That we forget we are here to do and to learn

And to spread the news of the new cosmic view.
The future's determined by me and by you.

This year, instead of just spreading good cheer,
By saying, "Merry Christmas!" or "Happy New Year!"
Instead of saying the words "Happy Chanukah"
I say "Bosnia, Somalia, and Nicaragua."
I say "Think of the homeless, the wastes of our wars."
I say "Think of the innocent behind locked-up doors."
I say "Each child we love loves others when grown."
I say "Each seed we sow grows others when sown."
I say "Each act, when committed, is part of the whole"
And "The New Age is coming to each New Age soul."

Two

The Star of Bethlehem!
The ancient prophets had cast the spell...

Take a deep breath...
Put yourself in the ancient mindset...

'Tis easily done.

Imagine yourself in the Hills of Galilee.
    Back then, there were no planets in the sky!
        Not even a notion of a solar system...
            Only a million points of light.

Stars, stars, and more glorious stars!
    Each star a tribute to a Nameless God;

But some stars wandered round the heavens

And every other decade the Star of David appeared,
    An alignment of Jupiter and Saturn
        Signaling the birth of the new King.

The prophets studied the stars.
They held the secret of time.
They held the knowledge of calendars.
They held the awareness
of past and future.

For centuries, prophets watched the King Star.
They watched it wander
Through the Signs of the Zodiac,
Studied the cosmic relationships,
Paid homage to the Sign of the Fish,
The Ruler of their Holy Lands.

Their prophesy:

"When the Star of David appears
In the Sign of the Fish,
The King of Kings shall be born
And the Times Will Change!"

And so it came to pass that in the East,
Where Persians studied the Stars,
Three Zoroastrian priests
Saw the Star of Stars!

They saw the magnificence of their time,
Jupiter and Saturn slowly dancing
A cosmic dance to the heavenly music.

They saw them slowly approach each other in the sky.

Was it true?

Could it be?

Yes. Yes.

YES!

THE TIME HAD ARRIVED!!
The Great Conjunction would be in Pisces.

They spoke:
    "The Age of Pisces shall begin!
    It is the fulfillment of the prophecy!"

And meanwhile, in the Hills of Galilee,
    Others looked up,
        Saw millions of stars,
            Without the cosmic knowledge
                That this was the time.

The Bible tells us that the astrologers from the East
    Told King Herod that they had seen his star.

Herod knew that the astrologers knew!

Herod tried in vain to stop the great change,
But even the King could not prevent
The tide of events that were destined
To change everything.

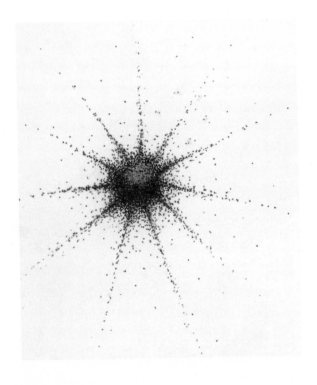

Three

The Lights grow dim and then go out;
The Inner Sky begins to shout!
The Light appears in Holy Sky;
The Star Shines down. "The Babe must die!"

King Herod speaks these words with fear.
When he knows the end is near.
Old prophets say the King of Kings
Will come and end all earthly things.

The wondrous Star of David sings;
The magic bell of Christmas rings,
When that star moves to sign of Fish
Mankind receives its special wish!

The prophets speak their words of power;
In Eastern lands, priests climb a tower
To watch stars' movements up above
And patiently wait for God's special hour.

Three Magi see a special sight!
They algebra all through the night.
The Great Conjunction, it draws near!
They must act now and get it right!

They journey toward the Holy Land.
With simple gifts for Child grand.
When Herod hears astrologers have come.
He summons the Zoroastrian Band.

The Magi show Herod the prophets' sign
Including Jupiter and Saturn in line.
They explain why they have come this far
And Herod knows he's run out of time.

When the end seems near, we get afraid
To leave the life that we have made.
Herod tries the holy child to kill
But is overpowered by the strength of God's Will.

ChristMass marks that time of year
When dark of night brings on the fear.
We light the light of lights once more
And Watch the Star in mind so clear

Four

A Christmas Wish...

As the sun slips into lower latitudes
And the Northern zones inch closer to winter
The air cools, the heart warms
And the HolyDay season comes round again!

Time of Love & Time of Cheer!
It's that special time of year

For Christian, Atheist, and Jew
For Muslim, Buddhist, and Hindu
For all the differences we've got
For what's in common and what's not;

We make the time to set aside
And celebrations open wide

Our hearts and souls to those we love
Both here on earth and up above.

Words, words, a flow of words
Soar o'er my head, like mighty birds…

With days so short and nights so long
Into the dark we sing our song

We sing of hope; we sing of praise
We try our best to spirits raise.

The Holy Spirit is the light
That shines so brightly through the night.

Beyond religion's narrow names,
Light is light, to all the same!

It's words that differ, not the good
That we all can do, as well we should.

The lesson at this time of year
Is basic, cosmic, and so clear:
Take some time away from stress;
Stand back from the human mess;

Set politics and beliefs aside;
Put away your ethnic pride.
Negativity and judgment, we don't need
For this is time to plant a seed.

A seed is like a little child;
Vulnerable, impressionable, and mild.

It needs love and encouragement to grow,
And warm protection from the snow.
This seed we plant in winter deep,
In mid-summer we shall reap.

It's a seed of thought that as times pass
Will turn to deeds that do outlast
Humanity's problems of war and hate.
These needless evils will abate
As we hold on to Truth's precious seed,
The word of Cooperation we will heed.

The earth, which used to be so great
Grows tinier as we communicate,
And now it's like a shrinking ball
With no room for war at all.

What happens in Afghanistan
Affects the folks in every land.

South Africa's Apartheid scheme
Polluted the planet with its stream.

As structures fell in the USSR
They gave a call both near and far.
They gave a call both far and near
For all humanity to hear;

For all humanity is but one!
All life depends on the light of the sun.
All life is holy: man, bird and beast.
To respect all creation is the very least

We can do as we journey through life,
Increasing happiness and reducing strife.

It's possible (you know) for peace to come
For war and hate to be undone.

It will happen not by global law;
This kind of thinking is a flaw.

Global change takes place in the heart
With each of us doing our own part.

So think a good thought;
    Sing a good song;
Mend an old friendship;
    Set right a wrong;

Plant seeds of love;
    Spread the good word;
Give more than you get;
    Haven't you heard?

The more you give;
    The more you gain;
It's natural law;
    It's very plain.

Every thing has reaction;
    Good & bad.
Pleasure & pain;
    Happy & sad.

You get back what you sow;
    You sow seeds & reap;
Plant fear & hate?
    Then surely you'll weep.

Watch what you plant;
  Care for your seeds.
Plant warmth and love;
  Sew kind, gentle deeds.

The Universe is a vast mirror of light,
And it reflects back... even at night.
In these longest of nights as I open my eyes
I see you and yours both healthy and wise.

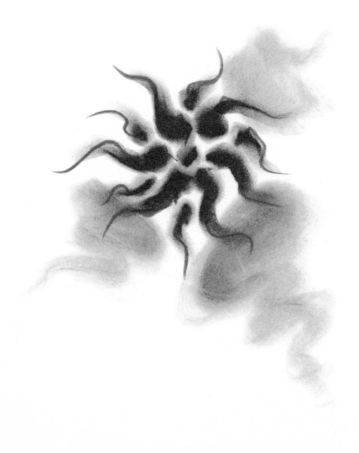

Five

Oh Bethlehem, the sleepy town
The wondrous light!
The thunderous sound!
The darkest night!
The Lord of Light!
It surely was a glorious sight!

Dark and light; Light and dark!
Only at night can we see a spark.
A glimmer of light; A glimpse of what's real;
To love and to cherish; to share what we feel.

Light and dark; Dark and light!
The Lord gives breath and shows us what's right.
In these longest of nights when the sun it is gone
There is thought of Him; He's second to none.
There is thought of his son and all that he's done.

Oh winter deep, all lined with gray
The lights, the sounds are here today.
The waters come, the trees they grow,
The thoughts we share, the seeds we sow;
The waters freeze; the snows blow cold;
The past comes back; the tales are told
From times gone by to times not yet,
Our dreams stay dry; our lives get wet.

The tiny earth goes round in space
While we humans run our race.
We think we know what's going round,
Our feet, we think, are on the ground,
But when we finally learn the score
We see that there is so much more.
The earth, immense, each day grows small
The teeming masses heed the call

Of freedom's urge, too strong to kill;
Of tyranny we've had our fill;

Watching brothers in foreign lands
Throw off the grip of iron hands

As iron curtains disappear
Global peace becomes so clear

For war is caused by governments
And the building up of armaments

Not by folks like you and me
Who only want to feel they're free.

With TV, radio, and music around
Even peasants in China know freedom's sound.

In dark places under tyranny's fist
Plain folk confront with what they have missed.

Democracy: the vision of Jefferson and Paine
Has spread wildfire o'er the plain;

Washed to the sea by the early spring rain
In far away places, it rises again

Like the ebb and the flow of the ocean's great tide
We humans are only along for the ride;

But at times, so few (yet they do exist),
We can put our foot down and strongly resist.

We can redirect even the ocean, so strong
And say beyond doubt, "This is not right, it's
wrong!"

Take control of your tide! Be cause, not effect!
Be like Jesus of old, when he started a sect;

A few followers at first, a small, humble start
But the words were so true and they hit the mark.

Russian, Czech, Chinese, and Pole
We're all part of a greater whole

Christian, Atheist, Jain, Hindu
Buddhist, Mormon, Moslem, Jew

From every corner of the world
We see the flags proudly unfurled

Declaring that, at last, we're free!
A consciousness called humanity!

The sum of every child, woman, and man
Each playing out a cosmic plan,

For life is a stage;
We play our part;
We think with our head;
We feel with our heart;
We pray with our soul;
We see with our eyes;
We sink to the depths;
We soar through the skies;

We live life and love, this I do know,
But at this time of year when the sun sinks so low
A dimension is added from way in the past.
One man is remembered whose deeds seem to last.

It matters not if you're Christian or Jew
To see that Christmas can mean something to you.
It can mean that, though we have a short time on
earth,
There is something more, beyond our net worth,
Beyond what we have, beyond what we do,
Beyond the material, we can learn to see through.

We can feel the spirit of a time gone by,
For two thousand years is the blink of an eye.
So, at this special time of year
Take time and listen to what you hear.

Do you hear the sounds of capital gains?
The rules of religions binding like chains?

Or do you have a wider vision of things?
Do you know the real meaning of the King of Kings?

This time of year, this day of rest,
When wise men journeyed toward the West,
They followed his star, the sign from above,
To shower the babe with the power of love.

We share in his love, we bask in his glow
We all have each other—that's all that I know.

I know this is truth, and oh! one thing more…
A truth handed down from days of yore,
A truth handed down from times of old,
A truth worth its very own weight in gold:

Some things are big, some things are small,
Together they make up something called "all."
All that there is below and above
Is connected by God, and sometimes called "love."
All that there is above and below
Is one and the same, this I do know.

And on Christmas Evening when the sun has gone down
We get on our camels and ride into town.
We bear gifts of spirit and bundles of love
And sing praise to the Glory of Heaven above!

Six

'Twas the years before Two Thousand
    and all over the place,
The planet was suffering
    from the human race;

The recycling bins were stacked
    by the curbs with care,
But without gas for the trash trucks
    it would forever sit there;

And I in my fervor
    and incurable hope
Had just about reached
    the end of my rope.

I heard from a friend
    that the end was so near.
I could take it no more,
    so I turned a deaf ear.

I was tired of hearing
    bad news on TV,
So I closed my eyes tightly
    and tried clearly to see...

I saw the whole picture as plain as could be
Things that eyes opened just never could see:

I saw Arabs and Jews living side by side;
I saw an end to the mass genocide;

I saw a planet where concern for our friends
Was more important than driving a Benz;

I saw the Iron Curtain come tumbling down;
I saw enemies join hands and dance around;

I saw a time and a place where everyone had
A home and a meal and I was only too glad;

For we'd worked ourselves into an unworkable place
Like rats running around in a crazy rat race;

Where politicians had taken from all of us folks
The feeling of power, but it's only a hoax

'Cause I saw revealed as I closed my eyes
A very clear vision of paradise.

Technology flourished, but no longer for war
Once we decided peace was worth fighting for.

We fought with our hopes and fought with our dreams
And political wars fell apart at the seams.

Political problems need solutions, not hate.
Death on the battlefield's an unacceptable fate.

But back to my vision of Heaven on Earth
'Cause I saw it for real and I know what it's worth.

I saw enemies talking about things of concern
And admitting they knew not which way to turn;

Admitting they'd worked themselves into a hole
And things had grown quickly out of control.

Admitting the fate of the whole human race
Was caught up to its neck in a wild goose chase

Of tribal boundaries and claims of material wealth
While Planet Earth was suffering from ill health.

These enemies each had a vision like mine
Revealing to them that there wasn't much time.

Electronic technology has cast a new net
Across the whole earth and we're all getting wet;

For the flood that occurred in the Biblical Age
Is happening again with a frenetic new rage,

But this time the waters don't fall from the sky,
There seems to be a new modus operandi.

The waters of human emotions run deep
And now they are flowing to make a clean sweep.

With the widespread use of radio and TV
People all over know other people are free,

So they refuse to accept a lesser role
And will do anything to reach their goal.

It's the same thing that has gone on for so long.
But technology's singing a very new song.

A song where emotions can release chemical death
That are carried by winds to poison your breath;

A song where a rocket can be guided by heat
And lay a warhead right at your feet;

A song where one country must get along with the rest
And there's no room for discussions about who is best;

Technology 's singing a soft requiem
For anyone who thinks there's an us and a them.

The media has shrunk this planet so small
That there's no room for misplaced emotions at all.

Dams cannot hold back the fire of hate
We must channel aggression before it's too late.

In days of old when someone got mad
They just hit someone else, and although that was bad,

The damage they did was local and slight
Now technology spreads hate like a streak of black light.

Psychic infection is worse than Black Plague,
And although this concept might seem a tad vague

It's more important now than it was ever
'Cause the whole planet is out on one end of a lever.

All the bad vibes are on the other end
And no one knows what is around the next bend.

We can help right now in our own little way
By making the right little choices today.

We can choose to fight this forest fire of hate
By controlling our own brush fires before it's too late.

We each contribute to the greater whole.
We clean up the world as we clean up our soul.

If we eliminate wars amongst family and friend
It would grow and soon larger conflicts would end.

Now if this all seems like Pollyanna gone wild
Just look into the eyes of a babe, new and mild.

See the future before us as the past fades away
And make a resolution on this New Year's Day.

Say aloud with me and a million others, too:

> *I know what I want and I know what to do.*
> *I choose on this day to promote peace and love.*
> *I look into my heart and to stars up above*
> *As I take this oath for once and for all*
> *To do what I can, no matter how small.*

As another year fades right into the past
Remember that even these times won't last.

So have a holiday season that's the best one so far
And give some thought to how lucky you are!

Seven

Peace on you and peace on me;
In my dream, it's this I see:

'Twas the decade of change and all over the earth
A new human vision was ready for birth.

And I, in my own way, had just settled down
To write all about what I see all around:

I see resistance and its fears,
The grief of war with painful tears.

Africa, Asia, even L.A. —
Is hateful violence here to stay?

I shout "no" with firm belief,
Then breathe a sigh of great relief
And send this poem into your mind
With a peaceful image, well defined.

This year at Christmas, it's the same;
Two thousand years we've played this game,
A game remembering a man in the past
Whose god-like deeds through ages last.

Whether you're Christian, Muslim, Hindu or Jew,
The deeds of Jesus are known to you.

Although his message was of high love.
We forgot that it came from heaven above,

So we turned it into a church-full of rules
And armies of soldiers acting like fools.

Crusaders of God, with fear in their hearts;
Soldiers defending territorial parts;
Soldiers of Nations with invisible gates;
But the boundaries are falling, in spite of our hates.
When things change too fast, we sometimes hold on
To things in the past that have already gone.

The past is our key to security
But now it's time to let it be.

If you see peace on me and peace on you
Then it's peace that will shine through!

Some people call this "to affirm"
(I have no problem with this term.)
Some people call on Jesus' name
Some use Buddha, it's the same.

You plant that seed from up above.
You picture inner peace and love.
You cast out historic fears and hate;
But do it now, it's getting late;
Do it now, before life quakes;
Do it now, make no mistakes.

Right now is time to plant the seeds
To overgrow hate's spreading weeds.

Each thought of joy, each thought of peace
Puts overt hate on the decrease.

When your heart fills with spirit light
It spreads throughout this longest night.
But Christ's mass is not the only way
To celebrate a holy day.
From every culture on this earth
Traditions show us what love's worth.

The natural rhythm ebbs and flows
Life force swells; with death it goes.
Walls get built and then they fall;
Slaves are freed and then stand tall;
Nations fall; new nations rise
This goes on before our eyes.

What we think is permanent, forever,
Changes with the changing weather.
Belief systems, too, change with time
And herein lies a key to my rhyme.
We live in times of major change
Where basic truths do re-arrange.
More choices, more gains, and more to lose—
It's oh so simple but gets so confused.

As confusion increases, and uncertainty gains,
We try to minimize all of our pains.
Buddha taught that sorrow begins in the mind,
That pre-conceived notions tie us in a bind.

Mohammed, Krishna, and Martin Luther King
All taught, in their own way, the very same thing.
Abraham, Moses, and Lao Tze
Each had the very same thing to say.
John Lennon asked us to give peace a chance;
Gandhi lived peace, yet took a firm stance
Against the fundamental beliefs of his day
To bring about change in a non-violent way.

Sing of this change with voices high,
Think of the star and reach for the sky;
Think of the peace that resides in your heart,
Stop the insanity, it's now time to start.

Peace on you and peace on us all,
The Millenium's here, and the future does call.

Eight

Regardless of one's religious beliefs,
    in the West, time is measured
        from this cosmic event
            two thousand years ago.

Two thousand years ago
    the course of history was altered.
        The planet was changed.

Even today, we count the years
    from this Great Conjunction
        of Jupiter and Saturn
            in the Sign of the Fish.

The Church acknowledges the symbolism of the Fish.
    This, after all, was the Age of Pisces.

Ages pass,
    and now,
        in the years around the New Millennium,

We look back twenty centuries
    to remind ourselves
        of the Eternal Glory
            of Universal Love
                and Light.

We remind ourselves of the Great Conjunction!

We remind ourselves that these, too,
    are Times of Great Proportion.

We remind ourselves that the New Age
    begins for each person
        at a unique time,
            and that the time
                is now ripe
                    for many.

We remind ourselves of our cosmic history.

We reconnect with our past.
We remember the ancient prophecy.
We reconnect with the stars of change.
We are like Noah, each of us.
    And the Waters are here!

The Flood has returned!
The Biblical Proportion is upon us!
    But now it is different.

The Waters are in the Air;
    The Feelings are on the Airwaves;
The Water Bearer is Aquarius;
    The waves are electromagnetic.

The Flood of Images is out of control.

Our minds are drowning in a sea of thought-forms.

Our population is swimming
    in a phantasm of violence.
Image-makers play on fear,
    and people are killed in the streets.
Technology is out of control,

We have lost our soul.
We have reached the dark night and we are lost.
We have arrived at the deepest night of winter.
Many see no hope for the future of mankind.
Many fear the end is near.

Species are becoming extinct at alarming rates.
Our forests are vanishing;
Our fish are disappearing;
Our waters are sick with poisons;
Our food is chemically altered;

Our minds are filled
    with sensational Hollywood images,
But our brains are linking
    through cyberspace in powerful new ways.

Computers are reaching
    through the dark of darkest nights
            as electrical nervous systems spark
                connections in the air.

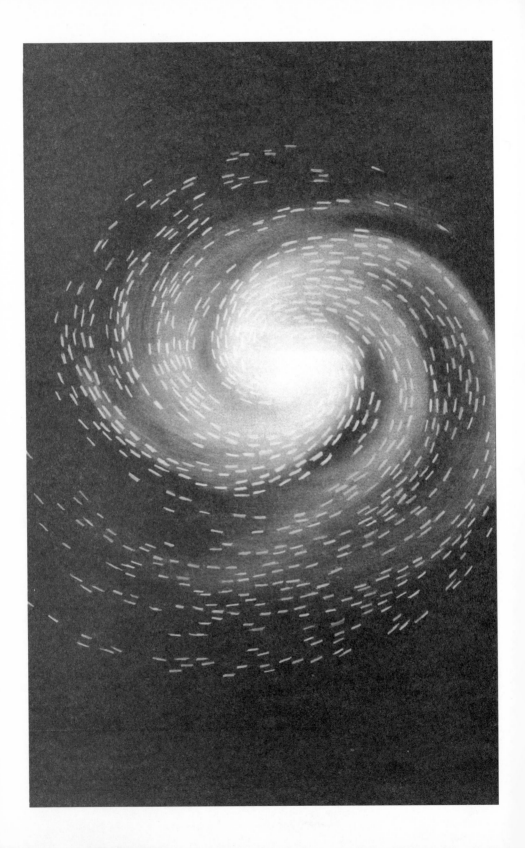

Inter-networking brains
   make their own virtual reality
      without regard for ideology
         or nation-state
            or politicians.

On self-survival mode,
   Planet Earth creates its self-awareness.

Electromagnetic waves wash the planet clean.

Waves of Love are stronger than waves of fear.

Waves of Life & Waves of Death
   rock on endless seas of time.

Nighttime is Death.
   Now it is the Time of the Soul.
Christmas is the Celebration of the Longest Night.

The Light goes away,
   and naturally, the Light returns!
The message of Christmas
   is the message of Solstice.

In the Deep Dark of Night,
   there is a Holy Light!!

Miracles happen by Cosmic Decree!

When ego steps out of the way,
    we recognize Selfhood.
Without ego in the way,
    Jesus approached Godhood.

This time of year,
    we pop out of our time/space boundaries.

We jump back in time to the birth of a child.
We rekindle the Magic of Cosmic Proportion
We light Festive Candles!
We celebrate Miracles of Light!

This time of year, we each become a Holy Child.
This long night rebirths the potential
    of the babe in each of us

And we remember that real gifts are gifts
    of light and love;

And we remember that William Blake wrote,
    "I have tried to make friends by corporeal gifts
    but have only made enemies.
    I have never made friends
    but by spiritual gifts,
    by severe contentions of friendship
    & the burning fire of thought."

Christmas is the celebration of a Cosmic Event,
    An astrological marker in the year
    and in the millennia.

Christmas is part of a rhythm of social change.
Every year, we celebrate the Miracle Star;
    The Old Jupiter/Saturn Conjunction.

But today, we also celebrate the New Christmas Star!

Saturn, Uranus & Neptune conjoined in Capricornus:
    The Goat of the Mountains.

This Light Shines through this dark of darkness;
This Light Shines in Present Times;
This Light is known by the Magi of our Times;
This Light is defining the Great Changes;
This Light is calling to the future;
This Light is the Light of the Millennium.

As in Biblical Times, we each play our part
We find inner light and project it into outer darkness.

Hold your spiritual candle high,
   in all its quiet luminosity,
   in all its magnificent glory,
   in recognition of the magic of the cosmos,
   in awe of the One Spirit
   in remembrance of that Star;

And Throughout the Land Proclaim:

Peace on Earth
   and
      Good Will to All.